The Book of Catapults

David J. Rothman

ISBN-13: 978-0615754185

Catapult drawing from "Dictionary of French Architecture from 11th to 16th Century" dated 1856, is in the public domain in the United States. This applies to U.S. works where the copyright has expired, often because its first publication occurred prior to January 1, 1923

White Violet Press
1840 West 220th Street, Suite 300
Torrance, California 90502

Acknowledgments

Poems from this manuscript, some in earlier versions, have appeared in the following journals:

Agni: "Apollo to the Athletes"
The Atlantic Monthly: "Not My Leg"
The Café Review: "Birdsong and the Old Night," "What Must Be Done Again Today"
Calapooya Collage: "Admire Sandburg"
The Chiron Review: "Dandelion," "Too Much Talk"
The Christian Science Monitor: "The Shape of Water Most Like Love," "Camembert"
The Edge City Review: "Alma Mater," "Joe," "Jacob Asleep"
The Formalist: "Paradise Valentine"
The Gallatin Review: "Theories of Decay"
The Gettysburg Review: "The Year of Wind," "Bird, Beast, and Flower"
Harvard Magazine: "A Man Is a Wolf"
Hellas: "The Unicorn"
The Journal: "The Avocado"
The Kenyon Review: "Breaking the Jug"
Literary Imagination: "The Owl and the Nightingale"
Lucid Rhythms: "The Next Poem I Will Read Is 'Justified'"
New Mexico Humanities Review: "Selling Brellazum"
Orphic Lute: "An Apology for Poetry," "A Neighbor"
Plains Poetry Journal: "A Letter Home"
Poet Lore: "The Turn Things Take"
Poetry: "One of the Lords of Life"
Sparrow: "New York"
Think Journal: "The Death of the Chair," "Building an Alphabet"
Unsplendid: "Something Goes Wrong," "The Rock"
The Wallace Stevens Journal: "It Is Spring"

Other poems appear in the following books:

> *Dominion of Shadow:* Photographs by Allen Brown, poems by David J.
> Rothman. Buena Park, CA: Gardner Lithographs, 1996: "The
> Child."
> *The Geography of Hope: Poets of Colorado's Western Slope.*
> Ed. David J. Rothman. Crested Butte, CO: Conundrum Press:
> "One of the Lords of Life," "The Shape of Water Most Like Love."

Some poems previously published have been reprinted in other journals:

> *Powerful Currents:* "The Shape of Water Most Like Love" (from *Th
> Christian Science Monitor*)
> *Mountainfreak:* "The Shape of Water Most Like Love" (from *The
> Christian Science Monitor*)

The composer Michael Pelz-Sherman has set "The Shape of Water Most Like Love" to music, in a piece of the same title which was premiered in Crested Butte, Colorado, as part of the Western Slope Chamber Music Series (now the Crested Butte Music Festival). The performers included Suzanne Ash, soprano; Harvey Harriman, baritone and narrator; Amy Muller, piano; Jim Horton, viola; Veronica Berkes, flute; and David Johanssen, trombone.

"Goodbye to Greenpoint" received High Commendation in the Margaret Reid Poetry Contest for Traditional Verse.

"The Death of the Chair" received a commendation in the Cecil Hemley Memorial Award from the Poetry Society of America, "for a lyrical poem on a philosophical theme." Judge: Elizabeth Socolow.

***

Translations of Dante's Divine Comedy are taken from Allen Mandelbaum's *Inferno* (1980), *Purgatorio* (1982) and *Paradiso* (1984), all in the Bantam Classic edition.

Table of Contents

3 / The Shape of Water Most Like Love

The Book of Catapults

Just give me one more chance.
I know I can temper my faith in the book of catapults,
My obsession with sunlight on a dial,
My joy in the enchantments of this theodolite,
And attend instead to our mortal days.

Breaking the Jug

I held the gallon jug in my right hand,
One finger curling into its mouth like a question,
And I hurled it at the wall. It had a decent heft,
The unsurprising sense of a thing as it is.
It was not a beautiful jug, or old,
No more valuable than the jug we break
Whenever we open our eyes.
A little wine roiled in the bottom,
Dregs of the past.
The jug floated like a small green cloud,
Ruling the apartment's gray, bare sky.
When it touched the wall
There was a moment when its axis
And the gigantic axis of the world
Crossed for the last time, like swords.
Its cheap seam glinted tragically,
As if somehow things could be different.
Then the jug blew apart under the impact of laws
That flood out into life like dust from a star.
The almost empty jug and the final drops of wine
Scattered, soared outward like a busted paradise,
Fulfilling equations of gravity and momentum
As they came to a mosaic rest.

We lay spattered with wreckage, laughing.
The room was bathed in the continuing light
Of an afternoon. As shadows slowly traveled
Away from themselves, the brilliant shards
Sparkled like the traffic coursing the streets below,
Each shoe and hubcap searching for that destination
Where it might join again with light and love
And thereby return to its senses.

1 / A Man Among Beasts

Ahi quanto a dir qual era è cosa dura
Esta selva selvaggia e aspra e forte
Che nel pensier rinova la paura!

Ah, it is hard to speak of what it was,
That savage forest, dense and difficult,
Which even in recall renews my fear.

Inferno 1.4-6

Apollo to the Athletes

Imagine your bodies pouring into time
Until all that remains is ordinary life.
The nights, however wonderful, however filled
With work and dollars, love and service, will swim by
With no further dream of jamming the hoop,
Of landing blindly on the balance beam
As if you were a gyroscope, of running
Into the cheers of emptiness, of one day tangling
A javelin in my spokes. My greater light will beat
In waves on lanes of water, rings of cinder,
Sculpted grass, punctuated snow, wood planks that glow,
Lined ice, raked clay, flat mats, cracked stone,
Patient stacks of numbered iron, the sandy pit
That provokes you like a taunt, and I will reveal them
In the perfection of their growing difficulty.
The blue, excluded sky, your receding limit,
Will frame everything with season after season
Of decline as you move slower and more slowly.
I will roughen your skin, burn into your joints,
Unstitch your guts, pull back your gums and dry your sex.
I will wheel my infinite fire around your heads
With the indifference of a stone clock
And then I will blind you with a spike of ice
And scatter you under the feet of faster, stronger others
Until your efforts are less than history.

Wait, it gets worse. Perhaps the reclining horizon,
Where all the records surround you with expectations,
Has already turned its back on you forever.
You never know — this could be the afternoon
You take a bad hit, or your knee fails on its own
With a little chuckle,
Or your will abandons you for greener fields.
How sad it would be to watch all that work

Break into pieces as you were carried off the field.
I have seen it happen many times.
So, man and woman, put aside your pride.
There is no reason you are the fortunate ones,
Chosen to parade within the circle of the shapes and numbers
That define your hopes. It could have been another.
Remember your sweat cools only your own back,
Pushes away no darkness, adjudicates no truths.
You strut and preen while bullets fly.

O my athletes, now you are angry. You terrify me,
With your puny rage and training. None of you
Has the slightest grace of claw or wing,
None of you can swim the world while singing,
None of you can drive my car
With the cat, the hawk, the shark, and the spider,
And yet you are angry, and your anger sparkles
Like the tiny stars above my crown.

This is why I favor you and your record-breaking failures —
You cannot help yourselves, you understand my threats.

So armed, now go for it — make a shape in the world.
Cup your hands and raise cold water to your lips
One last time as you plan and stretch.
Then figure pain and pleasure into strands of gold.
Speak to me with the aspiring bodies
Driven by your frantic, graceful spirits.
Unleash the music of your games,
The clutch of babbling, magical rules
That fill with cries of failure, camaraderie, and glory,
And without which I would not exist.

Not My Leg

Not my leg,
My lean, strong leg.
Choose any other part,
But please don't start
With my lovely leg.
I'd look bad with a peg.

Not my hand,
My articulate hand.
Please don't let it
Get torn or shredded.
Writing this book
Would be hard with a hook —
You must understand
I need my hand.

Not my eyes,
Dear God, not my eyes.
Don't poke them out,
So I grope about
Like Homer, Milton, Joyce.
If you have to be blind
To have such a voice,
I find
I want my eyes.

Not the urethra, not the anus,
The avenues that meekly drain us.
At least if they block, or get infected,
Please let it be quickly detected,
So a minimum of me gets cut.
Leave them alone,
My necessary thrones
Of pleasure and smut.

Not my body, my only body.
I know that the construction's shoddy,
Not built to last —
Someday it will lie in the past —
Still, I cannot restrain myself
From praying for my own good health,
Which some denying part of me
Believes should last eternally,
Although that only could hold true
For something out of nature's view,
And not my body, not my body.

A Man Is a Wolf

By ingenious analysis, a man is a wolf.
Then, infinitely, a man is not
What a wolf is not: an hour
Tracking the photograph of his own sadness.
A man is a sly, howling beast.
Further, in some sense, a wolf is a man,
So he lies down at night, sighing,
And tries to forget the moon's orbit.
By extension, then, a wolf is not what a man is not.
His tracks are not the endless flickers
Leaves make tumbling across the lawn.
A wolf, like a man, can only observe them.

But beyond this, a man is not a wolf.
Otherwise how could he sit alone,
Late at night, quietly crying,
Until his shirt sleeve darkens with tears
And all the lights of the city seem to sparkle
Even more brilliantly? And a wolf is not a man.
He gnashes some pest out of his fur
With delightful fangs. This is necessary.
Otherwise a man, clinking threaded bottle mouth
Against a glass's rim, would have to stand
And bite the iron window bars
As if he could not recognize a triangle.

Too Much Talk

This conference? Dull. And we're so near the ocean.
Too many ghosts stroll down these hotel hallways
Displaying open wounds, demanding justice.
Better the sea than history, now, always.

Why join a parade? Standing on the sand,
Hands empty, head bathed in the breeze, feet bare,
I'll hover at the edge of everything,
Watching the sun go down without fanfare.

Salt fronds and whips of weed float back and forth
At the sandy brink of talk, not far from here.
Ignoring commerce and the hot boardwalk,
Each wave sighs and fulfills its long career.

I will push back my chair and go there soon,
Ignore the waiter who is doing his best
To serve the diner who will touch nothing,
Not one sweet bite of carrot or duck breast.

I will go to the beach. I'll go there soon,
And standing still, I'll lay the whole day down,
Just give the day away, give it away,
Then turn, turn back, and get the hell out of town.

A Man Among Beasts

A cat's lecture punctuates the air,
Each claw burning with animal beauty.
I agree with everything he says.
I agree with the claws of a cat,
Which prove life is a game,
And the purpose of all thinking
Is a successful kill.
I stand to say my piece.
The claws of the cat, I begin,
Extend into the dawn like God.
A crow flaps up and flies off, laughing.

What you say is still so true,
A little fox points out to me,
That you could not possibly be a beast.
A thousand voices sing in every word,
He barks, and then, Excuse me, I know
This paw has offended, like imagination...
Or is it the denial of imagination?
But hear me! No truth, no proof
Can smother our perfections of midnight,
The little rabbits, chicken eggs, or, if you're lucky,
A whole chicken. And pleasure can pass
From night to night despite the most careful dog.
My lips are on fire, and my eyes and tongue
Are in love with lies, as everyone knows.
Thank you very much. He sits down.
The wolves whisper among themselves.

Silence. The animals are looking at me,
And sniffing the air with renewed curiosity.
So is it now I am a man. Who could have imagined
Such fine degrees of judgment, such pain and pleasure,
Such a lonely parliament?

News from Granada

– for Garcia Lorca

These were the stereotypes:
The jealous martial beauty
Of gypsy fights – a guitar –
The Alhambra – sweet smugglers –
Cante Jondo – but the sun
Knew these things as well as he
And it wanted deeper songs,
Of a man dead in the street
With a knife stuck in his chest,
Of a rose that seeks no more.

You will lie alone, darkness
Surrounding you, on your back,
And realize it is not light
You desire, or Spain, that place
Created by foreigners
To satisfy a style's need.
You will dream or remember
Blood, phantasmagoric guns,
The forms of endless travel
Over stony roads, blind seas.
Soon the morning will wake you
Filled with longing for something
As ordinary as shoes
That lie laced where they were kicked
Last night after laughter's coup.
Dawn plays across the leather,
Its dull creases like crow's feet,
Idiosyncratic curves
Of tired soles and heels – results
Of going to and fro, back
And forth, to look at a rose,
At the side of a building,
Into an old woman's face.

I died so terribly, pain
Charging up through my young guts
In the bullets. But confuse
The easy theme of evil.
Stand in the way of ideas,
Gripping a rose by the stem
And holding it out to them
As the blood drips from your fist.
Tell them, for all the good it will
Not do, about the sky, eyes
Still ravished by walking out,
The passionate end of time.

Theories of Decay: A Translation

Today's crocodiles have lost their bite,
And the mocking birds this spring
Are obviously faking it.
Where are the good old cowboys
Who used to dream of Delphi
And then hoist flags in their hair?
Following the ketchup
That meanders like the frontier
Across a plate of cheap eggs.
These days, let me tell you,
You can only trust your comments
To the whispering ears of reeds.
And even the rugs are argumentative.
But how wonderful bacteriology used to be!

There's no real plastic any more.
I ought to know. When I was a kid
You could kick words out of a cow
And laughter returned like a boomerang.
Now even the snow sounds like roses.
Before, pens and coughing lived together
In a neoclassical pose, and when they made love
They did not look in the mirror.

It's very sad. There are no more hydrobikes,
Lunar colonies, metadogs, or happy graphs.
Father, even theories of decay
Aren't what they used to be.

A Letter Home

Dear fa(r)ther:

I was walking to wo(e's)r(oc)k yesterday
When I saw this D(irty hodge-p)odge
(Of)D(ung, c)ar(rion, and)t(rash)
(Fe)S(tering and p)itting in a vacant lot.
You guessed it — this (s)car
Was the s(h)ame model
You gave me(mory) so long ago.

A For(bidden) Sal(v)e sign s(qu)at(ted) on the d(amp)ash.
It called back so much of(fal) — well, you know,
That (s)kid I once was, a pimply s(uppurating)elf —
And you as a young ma(levola)n(ce) —
Remember how we used to work on (b)it(terness),
The(ory's) (c)old (st)one, fix(at)ing it(s) (er)up(tions)?
Well, now I can bu(r)y you(r) (b)one(s) in r(ock)et(b)urn.

I just had to (be)get (w)it for you. I know you'll think
That what I've d(et)on(at)e(d) is extravagant,
But I hope you'll accept (sp)it as (f)a(te's) gift.
We can work on rebuilding (fr)i(gh)t together,
Just like in the (sp)o(i)l(e)d days.

The (st)ink is still wet on the deal
I signed with the ow(lish pun)ner,
A g(rinning a)u(thorit)y named S(a)tan,
Who, strangely enough, swears he(ll)
Is your friend from before the war(ts),
And that he'd like to (s)hear your voice again,
S(lash,)h(ack, and fl)ake your hand,
And chew over (m)old times.
He said (t)he(cosmos) hasn't forgotten
You(r) (f)at (p)all. He looked fat(al) and happy,

And kept saying "Now(ily, conscious will will) remember
To tell your d(r)ear(y), (fo)ol(e)d Dad
How I (d)am(n). But he'll know who (Meph)i(s)t(opheles) is.
Tell him I've thought of him (s)often(ing) over the years."

I gave him your (g)n(arled sl)umber.
(K)No(wing his) d(eterminati)o(n,
I wo)u(ld)b(e)t he'll call.
All's well here, everything the same.
Talk to you in a (dooms)day or two.
Say (s)h(r)i(ke) to mom.

      (G)Love,
               Your (poi)son,
                        (O)Ed

Birdsong and the Old Night

"Just before the dawn the songbirds sing
As if they are so happy to be alive,"
Mused some idiot who didn't know anything
About how little birds survive.

It had been raining and blowing hard all night.
The courtyard chestnut creaked before the wind.
Inside, there was bourbon. There was a fight.
We all made up, the crowd thinned.

Now the fingers of another dawn
Revealed familiar faces, enterprises.
We had pretended the past was done and gone,
Defeated by slurred deals and compromises.

Soon the sky was clear and crisp and blue
And we could smell the sea breeze flowing in,
Making the city sparkle as if new,
Which it was not. Subtle as a bulletin.

Still it was good, a moment in which a man
Might come to accept or begin to understand
Something, in the way a cat inscrutably can
Understand or not understand

Who knows what? For us, the worn coin
Of a mortal landscape
And an apartment's overstuffed ashtrays,
Smeared glasses, song, and laughter, flickering out.

Goodbye to Greenpoint

1.

Is it worth remembering
That silver paint was flaking
From the shed? Its rusting roof
Across whose ripples cats walked
Leisurely, with runny eyes?
The summer's dog days slouched in
Giving their endless lessons
On how to gossip and smoke.

I want to forget, forget
The gray and green tarpaper,
Fake siding, dirty red brick,
The warpwood slats and the words
Sufficient to name the walls.
The cheap irregular sheets
Of some red-painted metal
Men carelessly stapled up
Were such empty, blinding things.

The Good Humor trucks blared bells
Each afternoon, their engines
Whirring to save the delight
Of cold, sweet uselessnesses.
Nuclear stereos rocked
The boulevards, the old piers
Splintering and rotting out.

2.

A mop hangs from a window
That could begin a story—
Some new, boring tragedy
Of coke, cash, cars, girls, and guns—
Or, more likely, laundry lined
Day by day above the weeds
That thrive in cracks. The children
Play with sticky bats and dolls.
So now you realize we
Have come to Greenpoint, neighbor
Of paralyzing rivers,
And your guide remains silent.
I will maintain this silence.
Even as you read this page
I have forgotten empty lots
Of tangled junk, tethered dogs
Yapping in the dark for hours,
The jagged holes in the streets.

3.

I have forgotten it all.
It has all become perfect.
I say goodbye to Greenpoint.
Sporting purified disgust,
I leave the key in the door
And leave, opening a smile
In the pleasure of forging
The place into nothingness.
I will go to the mountains.

And I will forget the man
Who could not live in Greenpoint,
The soulless thinker who shrank
From those who were living there.
He makes ungrateful noises.
I will throw him in the sea.
He will float away, leaving
A rhyme in his place, a rhyme
For everything in Greenpoint,
Even the woman who beats
Her young son until he cries.

An Apology for Poetry

I apologize.
I thought we were in a foreign country.
I was inspired by the exotic landscape.
The jagged green mountains that framed
What I had believed to be Arcadia –
That scene seemed to make all of our gestures
Meaningful, precise, and accurate.
It's so much harder than I thought.

I'm sorry.
The music must have gone to my head.
The guitar, from which each note must be strongest
At the moment it begins, confused me,
Filling my body with notions of love
That were completely inappropriate.
I guess I wasn't paying attention.

I know I was wrong.
The sad truth of life is that, like cuisine,
It must be destroyed to be enjoyed, used up
In its own experience. And you're right, you're so right,
We must eat and live each day, each day,
So the question must be: how?

Please reconsider.
Those irresponsible bastard philosophers
Who crossed my path one night in the forest
Continue pouring moonlight into the room.
I thought they meant the night of carnival
Began tonight. I hear them calling to me, like wolves.

But it's my fault.
I didn't realize the words I had chosen
Revealed such a deep failure to listen.
Surely you will speak to me again?
With that mischievous look in your eye?
Just give me one more chance.
I know I can temper my faith in the book of catapults,
My obsession with sunlight on a dial,
My joy in the enchantments of this theodolite,
And attend instead to our mortal days.

One of the Lords of Life

Peace to all living things,
I scribbled in the log on Vulture Peak
Because time was short and it was true.
Then I stood, like any American, alone,
To be in that immense desert glow.
Down into dusk, the Hieroglyphics and the White Tanks,
The Big Horns, the Harquehalas, and the Bradshaws
Offered bent, brown rock, forests of saguaros,
And hidden life to the emerging stars.

Lampless, I turned and scrambled three-point
Down the chimney, blaze to blaze,
Until I met the saddle dirt,
Then bounded down a crooked trail
Into the darkness growing visible.

A whisper in the shape of a green branch
Lay before me. Wonder not, it said.
And so I did not wait, although it ruled the path.
I had no chance to stop and listen
To the quiet voices of my education.
Only when I landed on my right foot
One runner's pace above did it become
A sinuous emperor of emerald
Warming himself on a rock in the patience
Of silence, cunning, and exile.

Nature does not suffer decay: always new,
Unlike the memory on which minds turn,
It unfolds like emptiness.
One word, his name, sparked from nowhere
And sank into my foot.

A hand reached down, carved wings,
Then plucked my muscles with more light.
Too big for dinner, too sudden for his surprise
To coil up and rattle out an argument,
I jumped into the current of our doing.
Pebbles tinkled like dice
As I leapt over the fat green snake
Who squirmed silently beneath my soles
Like a piece of animal cactus,
And I did not fall, I landed with a gravel crunch
Between the cacti, unstung, miraculously erect,
No mouth of numbing ash, no broken ankle,
Below the double distance a rattler can strike.

Strange alteration in me. The fruit was praise.
Mojave Green: I do not think I missed my chance
With you, but took it where it lay —
As if I had the choice.
You are still prompting my words
Away from deep, high speculation
And into one breath after another —
The coincidence of dusk and sage,
The distant glow of Phoenix, and the dying sun.
As I climb slowly up into these thoughts,
Remembering my long, headlong descent,
On which I lost the trail, then found it again
And walked out from the mountains in darkness,
I see you turning, raising your head in cold curiosity
As I vanish beneath your jaw, and I hear you calling my name,
Although you are ignorant of it.

Something Goes Wrong

Something is always going wrong –
A twist, a turn, a day, a song.
No matter how wise you are, or strong,
The doorknob breaks, you don't belong,
You and your love don't get along,
You are Fay Wray, life is King Kong.
Something is always going wrong.

Something is always breaking down –
A car, a joint, a day, a town –
And falling heavily to the ground.
It's prom night and you've torn your gown,
Your hand winds up at the lost and found,
Your lover demands merely one pound
Of flesh, but it's your heart. The sound
Of laughter turns to choking. Things drown
In life at last, and don't come round.
Something is always breaking down.

Something is always falling apart –
If it's not the horse, then...but why even start
To try to describe how wheels blow out
On superhighways, a valve in the heart
Clogs up and stops, gentle doubt,
The model of all thinking, cracks, entire
Neighborhoods, cities, and then nations plunge faster
And faster into anger, hatred, and disaster?
The straits we swim are always dire.
Something is always falling apart.

Someone is always screwing up.
Someone is always dropping dead.
The cops are always showing up

After the bullet's in someone's head,
Or stomach, or throat, or violent bed.
Who can predict the next bloodshed,
The plot some genius has dreamed up
To rob the little corner store
Or turn his sister into a whore?
You think that's bad? There's always more
Where that came from, more than we can
Imagine, for the subject's Man,
And someone is always screwing up.

So, doctor, drink with me, come drink with me.
I'll buy this round. We will do it moderately,
Then, homeward bound, let's walk the city,
Whose curbs are ruled by cash and pity,
And, knowing things are for the worst,
And something always can go wrong,
And there's no cure once a bubble's burst,
Attend, attend, to the night's sweet song.

2 / Building an Alphabet

"Correte al monte a spogliarvi lo scoglio
ch'esser non lascia a voi Dio manifesto."

"Quick, to the mountain to cast off the slough
That will not let you see God show Himself!"

Purgatorio 2.122-23

Building an Alphabet

The world is bathed in light
Or darkness, it does not matter.
For at my desk, alone,
Enmeshed in music and brutality,
I am an unemployed magician
Building an alphabet.

Anger is an ancient letter.
Anger that is truly anger
Insists on standing first.

The second letter is the first's Brother,
Belated body bound to anger.

Care is the brother of all letters.

Death does not care for letters,
But Denial is a letter.

O it is Excellent
To know the names of the letters
That never die.

Fear is an excellent letter
Because it quickens words with purpose.

God is the letter
That is not a letter.
Do not be afraid.

History is the letter
God made into salt.
Happiness is the rare letter
That leaves no history.

I am a letter
In history and happiness.

Justice requires all the letters
I am building.

Kindness is the letter after justice.
Or is it the letter before?

The Letter of the Law is the Law of Letters.
Love, a kind of Law,
Is not the Letter of the Law.
Love is the Letter of the Letters.

My Mother made me out of letters,
No less than law and love.

Number is the mother of all letters.

O is a number, and a letter,
And a word, and a fact
That cannot stop the alphabet.

O Pain is the letter
Shaped like a fetter.

You cannot Question pain
With a letter.

The letters Rule all questions.

Song rules all the letters.

Time is the song letters live within.

Time Utters its song letter by letter.

Vowels utter other, deeper letters
Within themselves.

My Wife lives within
Each vowel I utter.

Explanation is the wife
Of these letters,
Which cannot be explained.

And now here is the marvelous thing:
You cannot be explained with letters.

For now you are a Zoo
Of wild letters yourself,
Each clamoring to be fed first.

At last I have built an alphabet.
Little pieces of the world flash from its eyes.
What wonderful words I will write
With these magical letters!
The quick brown fox will jump
Over the lazy dog of forgetfulness,
For Alphabet, you are everywhere
And there is nothing you cannot remember.
O Alphabet, I love you.
Forget me if you can.

The Icicle

Like a tree triumphing over a nail,
The icicle had grown across the gutter,
Embedding it bite by slow, relentless bite,
Reached up and over, grabbed slate tiles,
And gathered at the corner spout's hole.
There each brick's nook, cranny, and crook
Yielded to the uniform logic of water,
Which gives ice muscles to crack rock,
Bend metal, sparkle, and sparkle with darkness.
Thicker than a man and shot through
With blue, white, black, and glassy clarity
That narrowed to a single, motionless finger,
It pointed its twenty-five foot body down
At trampled snow and the earth's center.
Liquid sunshine conspired with February's harsh evidence
To build ice out of slow time,
An ice joining touch, sight, and silence,
Except for the way a small breeze
Gusted around the corners. A great manifestation
Of winter, an architecture of magnificent patience
Dug downward into the evening's breaking fact.

And dug. The icicle absorbed the touch,
The eye, the silence, especially the eye,
Until sight became a thing changed, transformed
Into an empty greatness. Each perfect molecule,
Obeying its four laws, could not bridge
The gap between the ice and love.
No one had done this to song,
Or to the icicle. Instead, deep down,
Somewhere inside the icicle, a spinning sun
That drank all things into its eye

Had captured evening, air, and manifold icicle
Within an inarticulable grasp, broken things away
From their decorous places in any pleasure
Or pleasing memory of unasked, green questions.

No, within the gigantic king of icicles
There was no icicle, and no crown
Stood on the crown-like nonsense of ice.
No wing could be imagined to beat
Back up the great spike of thinking
Into flight. Less than a missing word
And more empty than an empty cup,
The icicle smashed, motionless, its own fact
Into less than pieces of dark glimmering,
Or stories in any genre. No mother,
No matter, could suckle such a famine
Of ice and deeper ice, ice signifying
Ice and the freezing isolation of seeing.

Was it a perfection of boyish play?
The icicle held no voices or ink
Up to that plea, took no authority
Upon itself to disprove the self-devouring facts.
The only winter, it gripped no syntax,
Nor a fact named cold, nor worked
From water, and would not answer queries
About its body, its likeness, its implications
And evaporating implications beyond, beneath, away, drowning
In the landscape of Boston and abstraction.
No human voice, or hand, no animal,
No green, spring stem, no mute rock,
No light, no darkness, not even yesterday
Brooded broken in the blank, perfect tense
Of that empty, unnamable god in February.

Deeper, darker, blanker, more shattered than marble
Under the numbing stamp of time's thumb,
The world tumbled down in fractal static,
Unsupported by the ground of any thing,
Any thought, any force that might work,
Open, build, love, make and make right
This immense loneliness into what could be.

Unpragmatic word that resonated nowhere but questions,
How fortunate you were, are, and become!
For it was only loneliness, loneliness without
Its name, big loneliness, boy, looking, hooked
Within you, for its name, finding yours,
And bringing it up into the air
That spoke in silent voices breaking open.
Loneliness, now named, deep in the icicle,
Turning after so many years and bowing
To the terrible world, is what cut
The insufficient bonds, unblessed the sophomore world,
Broke every word into animal sounds, unbuckled
Life from word from thing from love.
It was only loneliness, and under it,
Reborn, as true as any king icicle,
Was every lonely thing and word, fragmented
Out, signs of terrible, unborn, inward fires.

That infernal icicle pierced a thinking eye
With loneliness unnamed, afraid of itself, masquerading
Its gaps with ideas, but merciless, returning
Moment upon moment, growing inch by inch
Into an icicle. Only alone, it rippled
Down over itself, terrible, adult, alive, wordless,
Hissing angrily to be named and take

Its place above the other, quiet beasts.
Part of no eye's vocabulary, the icicle
That hung from Grays Hall in February
Shimmered in the lamplight, and prophesied silence,
The silence of each thing utterly alone,
Speaking only to itself, unmothered, unfathered, thought-
    embedded,
As if dirt and every friend's hand
Had to be perceived before becoming real.

But a you in loneliness makes loveliness,
And after and beyond the icicle returned
The Yard, the elms, the students, paths
Between the old brick, and the company
Of lovely others, although time took time
To build that insight out of loneliness,
The fact that had begun the work.
And time took time to turn up
That one word, loneliness, which was sleeping
In every meditation: the loneliness of thinking,
The loneliness of naming all the animals,
Of watching the Cambridge sky go purple
Then black in February, marking dark clarity
With no word that could couple it
To another's ear or eye, leaving imagination
Unfulfilled, screaking and scrambling in its loneliness.

False, painful prophet, ice Jeremiah, your gift
Was your savage, thorny shape, which revealed
Fragments talking to themselves, aspiring to touch
Defining love and faith against their gaps —
Loneliness that failed to devour what remained,

The signatures of others! For in purgatory
All things rise, flowing from unknown springs,
Even the man-child shocked into seeing himself
Alone in the contemplation of an icicle.

A Neighbor

1.

He speaks of having started a new life,
Of having cleared his late wife of decades

Out of his blocked mind, of therapeutic chants
That purge, of life's liberating dance and song,

But he lies. He can't get started again.
In the late afternoon, when his sobs

And moans drift down the banister, I
Have stood and listened to him cry out

Like an idiot parrot: "Janet I love you!
Janet I love you! Janet I love you!"

He breaks off in a stricken shout.
In the overheated stairwell I doubt myself

And what to do. His voice subsides
Into sobs and imaginings, collides with truth,

With time, with ignorance, the cold wall
Where no nightingales call or gardens grow,

"Alone, alone, alone!" he cries.

2.

                               Now key
In hand, I sit in my apartment. A cd lies

On the floor, ashamed. Like a pair of hands,
Two pigeons flutter into the bare

Branches of the chestnut tree.

3.

                           I meet my neighbor
The next day on the street.

He looks in my eye, asks how I am, puts one
Hand on my shoulder, calls me son. Bushy eyebrows.

I would tell him "An unexpected event will bring you riches.
A man knows how to sing

When he has to. At first
I thought the Chrysler Building nursed beauty

By rising into perfection. Late one Sunday night,
in streaming fog, each section

Of every gleaming ornament, the triumphant spire
Above the neon chevrons that only expire into daylight

Convinced me imprecisions should be denied.
I thought all stammered visions,

The inarticulate thing that tries to turn
Its way into words and burn our tongues

With too much, must
Be named as such —

A failure, mistake, undignified. But I was wrong.
There is no perfect song."

                                       But I cannot say a word.

4.

Sweet, living man! Pound the walls and floor, sing
Beyond any genius for your dead wife, bring

Her name through grief
Up here into belief,

And fill it with air.
Remember and testify to the dark scent of her hair.

However broken,
Let that love be spoken,

And weep for her in the indifferent dawn,
Pacing out the hours she is gone.

The Year of Wind

The year of wind fooled rivers of opinion.
People opened their mouths to speak on TV
But only laughter came roaring out.
So much laughter! Even in the street
The decorum of speech, in which all of us
Had become sad experts, broke down.
Accusatory fingers rose into the air
Like little monuments demanding time.
But thinking we were clouds,
Distant sails, doves wheeling away,
The two of us continued to live as before.
I didn't even bother to look
In the dead pig's eye as he lay
Sliced open from throat to anus
On the rickety table in the noodle shop.
So I didn't see what anyone could have seen.
My heart — only, after all, one ignorant pound —
Had finally been refined by a private love.
It burst its paper cage and flew off, cooing.

The Owl and the Nightingale

Owl and Nightingale went to a bar and drank,
Oh, they drank long and hard into the evening.
Nightingale eventually sang out:
Hour after hour down the dark winter bottles
Words become my spangled feathers,
Which rise forever with every singing lover,
Leaving behind old men who can only hear
Leaves crying, or not crying, on dry branches.
Owl, he said, Death is an old whore
Who will do anything for business. Ha!

To which Owl replied, with a generous gesture
Of his dark, peaceful wing, *Everything dies,*
Then sipped his beer.

Enraged, Nightingale perched on the pool table
And addressed the assembled drunkards:
Ladies and gentlemen, lovers, gods and goddesses,
Earthwalking pieces of earth soon to be earth again:
Even in the most perfect night
Neither dogs nor an infinite excess of stars
Can drown the name of a single hair.
No storm can lash true love indoors or underground,
No fact or wisdom can tweak the proof of love,
No anguished prayer or curse can buckle a song,
For every rose has always already found its name!
Every hand is haunted by a caress, only a word can say "no,"
And even that emptiness goes down like wine.
Even "Death" means "Yes!"
Even "Night" means "Love!"
Even "No" means "Maybe!"
Owl, you might be silently scudding our town,

But deep in every beyond of tonight's sweet bed
Burns another rocket of encrypted delight!

He pointed a delicate wingtip at Owl and laughed.
Owl blinked twice and said *Everything dies.*

Later, after the two friends had been forcibly ejected,
Nightingale chanted more sadly.
Dear Owl, he trilled, *I honestly thought my aria*
Back there in the bar would cheer everyone up.
But so what if I was wrong? Thank God you stayed with me,
To pick the utterly real gravel out of my forehead.

The street in which they found themselves coiled into the dark
As they searched for another bar among the snowdrifts.
Nightingale riffed drunk arpeggios as he flitted about,
While Owl hooted quietly on a bare branch, *Everything dies.*

Nightingale clung to a street sign and responded,
Yes, Owl, and so we might never stammer a living word:
The stars, the mud on the pool table,
The beauty of friendship —
But then how could we claim to sit around
Refusing everything and deaf to it all, eh?
Every word you make,
Every denial, is a form of my name.

Yet here it all is, Owl suggested,
In his calm, owlish way, looking stern,
Weighing Nightingale's life in his claws,
Here it all is, regardless of what you say.
Everything is here, without words, without you.
It concerns no one at all,
And is more open than night's horizon,

Greater even than me, and not what you think —
For everything dies. Nightingale, dear sweet friend,
Your beautiful song is only my descendant.
Everything dies. Everything dies. Everything dies.
To-who, To-who, To-who, he sang,
And guided Nightingale home through the dead of night.

Where, awaiting dawn's aureole,
Nightingale dipped his battered wing in ink,
And wrote these words.

Camembert

She wept as she sat in the restaurant
And ate sweet, perfect camembert alone.
She did not smile and neither did she speak —
And yet tear after tear rolled down each cheek,
Each filled with concentrated, tender pleasure
That only those small bites of cheese could measure.
How strange that something so unnecessary
As deliciousness should move her in this way —
The little pieces of milk, soft, pale, and darling
From some small unknown farm up to the north.
Still, she sat at that table thoughtfully,
With that hour's one true purpose, to taste cheese,
That she would then select for one month's menu.

It was her work, and no great crisis, no.
And yet the moment conjured something more.
But why go looking there, into the past?
Isn't it enough that eating is
Much more than need, and that for her, the boss
Of joy beyond the mere day of survival,
This morsel on this afternoon was better
Than any food need ever, ever be?
Her taste a kind of gratitude, or prayer
Intensely concentrated on the tongue,
And with that joy now to a purpose tied,
She finally put down the knife and fork,
Wiped off her lovely lips with a blue napkin,
Picked up a pen lying idly by her hand,
And under "Cheeses," wrote it: *Camembert.*

Selling Brellazum

Today the wind blew rain into wild knots.
In battered trashcans and dirty gutters they
Lie mangled, broken, bent, the cheap, shiny cloth
Unspindled from the fish-thin ribs. Big moths
Struck down by lightning, they lie splayed on the ground.
Discarded, spangled with drainage, spent, pressed flat
Like flowers in a book, or the chalked outline
Of a murder victim on the news, they clutter
The orderly prospect every transaction offers.
But out of Senegal, in airplanes, poor,
Alive to the streets, a bunch of fellas come.
Under empty skies it's watches, scarves, and hats.
When it rains they bring out other cardboard boxes,
Stack them carefully, display their wares
In a row on top, and stand in doorways, saying
Brellazum brellazum brellazum brellazum...

Alma Mater

Why should you have to give them up again,
The cold sun roaring up the hill and over
To paradise, a skating rink plowed clear
Each day for a puck's swift hop, and the little river
Rough frozen too far up itself to skate
And make it home before the day goes back.

What is the future of that growing lack,
Where fairgrounds' stamping, gambling hooves each fall
Beneath the canopy of dying elms,
And graceful lust with which the spring held you
And educated your cars without oblivion,
Combined in summer's ritual big splash.

Upon whose orders have you sought to smash
Your town hall, architectural school of kitsch,
Its little battlements for little battles,
Like fistfights in the defunct junior high
Some of you won and others, silent, lost.

And tell me, do you think you can exhaust
The dark that still sparks long, perplexed embraces
Up on Res Road as the ox-bow slowly rises
Through spring to flood the rich fields with tomorrow,
And trains that rode the rickety tracks to Canada,
Passing you by with two black whistles that set
On everything but did not insist on knowing.

How can you say it died when in its going
It trilled and scribbled itself everywhere,
Like Berkshire roads meandering through woods
In the perfection of a slow dissolve to weeds.

Sing bold denials from Round Hill to Leeds,
Beneath the rolling hills, for everyone!
The Red Lion Diner will always be the place
To talk about love, smooth elbows on the table,
Sweet drink in a ribbed glass, your bodies bodies
Of tigers, or close enough for jazz, so why,
Why give up the ghost of home in your mind's eye —
Though who could be so foolish as to think
There is a choice.

Joe

I was a boy and I remember you
As on your rusting one-speed bike you popped
A wheelie that went on almost forever,
Dropped only grudgingly to gravity.
So charmed, you charged away from town and school,
On West Street, which slopes gently down, then rises
Into the Berkshire Hills, an invitation
To get out that you no doubt one day took
Or maybe not, staying in town forever.

Your long black hair flopped in and out of your eyes
With copacetic finesse as you smacked open
The rest room door with one flip, wiry shoulder
And dove into that sanctuary, hawk-like,
Instead of answering the Principal
With words, leaving him standing by his office,
Jangling the change forever in
His polyester pockets. That was great.

Joe, what a name, and you were so hot, cool,
A flock of fists, curses and working problems,
In the face of what? Did you have parents, home?
Or did you live, without a past or cause,
Beneath a dank bridge in a shack, alone,
Smoking stolen cigarettes for dinner
And hatching no plans whatsoever, none,
Except to kick an open locker closed,
Hard enough to bend it, and then shrug,
Set for a fight; and to perfect that wheelie,
Unreeling it beyond your life's tough shambles
Into a thundering, stereo yes.

The Death of the Chair

The chair that stood by, idly, as a chair,
And once rubbed up, day after now gone day,
Against the dinner table, until a pair
Of parallel indentations worked their way

Into the edges of its back, is dead.
The shining grain craft warped into a shape
Appropriate for ease or stacking, wed
To place after place, room after room, landscape

Of conversation after conversation,
Meal after meal, word after word at a desk,
Has disappeared from every state and nation
Into a game that makes its name grotesque.

The smudged, bent X of tubular metal legs
That crossed under the seat is now a fire,
Or bird of paradise, searching the dregs
Of language for an allegory's attire.

The gentle stops at those leg ends, and the square
Of rubber that fit over each leg and filled
The space between the leg and seat of the chair,
To steady it, made a nostalgia that killed —

Yes, our gratuitous pleasures of the thing
Held out no chair. Even the chair of air,
The word-wood growing there, the first place-spring
Of maple, copper, and rubber was a snare

Of lethargic fact, speaking in tongues. It led
Inevitably back, back to the ease
Of clarity and control, a Procrustean bed
Of truth, back to the metaphor of disease.

What is required is to accept the death
Of things and turn back to a chair that is
Becoming another chair, becoming a breath
That means only another breath, a fizz

Of spattered ink and new chairs changing magic
Into tomorrow, pleasure into change,
The world into the virgin bride of tragic
Developments. Then you too will be strange

To the pain of living, strange to the past and strange
To the danger of the past, its hatred and care.
Yet here we are, and we are alive. So strange
To live, to think of you, to sit in the chair.

New York

Whitman! too bad you're not alive, quick, weird,
Chanting universal adhesiveness
Across the rooftops of our loneliness.
America could use your Gnostic beard.
Leave me alone! I never volunteered!
We squeak, I'm not responsible for this mess!
Preaching democracy in your rough dress,
If you heard this, you'd call out...Don't be scared.
Your life was just one life, like any other.
Yet you held hands with lonely, war-torn boys —
No fear could stop your democratic noise.
And your flawed recitative revealed the sea
As more than self or death. You were a brother
To each of us, and to infinity.

Bird, Beast, and Flower

Because there is always more of it
Pouring into the tiny void,
The sun outshines its singular paradox.

You can wash your hands of God or Broadway,
But sunlight, which is like mud,
Cannot be wiped away like mud.
The water is a sleeping lion.

Darkness is a spark of sunlight.
The word *no* blossoms like a small star
At a certain distance from the sun,
Which grazes on space like a herd of zebras.

The sun is both like silence, and, in silence,
Works its way across the houses
Of those you love, illuminating them.
Regard it only with your mouth open.

The sun is as solid as the stones
Upon which it beats,
The sun flies over every swallow
That arcs like the sun,
The painter, like the sun, leaps
Into the emptiness of a sunny street,
And daylight proves itself as true
As the tree it makes
Possible from one moment to the next.

Let the fountains of meaning rust,
Let anger, run dry and rot —
The sun is a fountain, everything else
The garden of its evident work.

The Prophet, 2 AM

Hibiscus blossom of obscure origins,
Twelve hours ago you were but a nipple.
Now you press your furled sail into a black sky,
A small, pink cigar smoking with promise.
You feather the darkness like a voice.
Every word whose past is missing
Finds its place within your throat.
Tomorrow I will crawl from bed
And descend to find you speaking,
This page, doormat to a vitality
Words cannot convey, spread at your feet.
Then tomorrow evening you will fade
With the certainty of a fireworks.
In the sun you will have been a small sun,
Under clouds you will have had to invent the sun.
The following day, a gardener of obscurities,
I will come from bed again,
Descending to find you wilted,
Five red stamens still protruding
From your closed tip. Then I will pluck you
At the base of your short, moist stem
To bring forth more, which is what
You have been offering from the beginning
Although you have no words yourself
And no words can ever become you
The way you did yourself, hibiscus blossom,
Ancient mallow whose origins remain obscure.

The Unicorn

The sentence "Unicorns do not
Walk, gallop, canter, run, or trot,"
Is true, because their soft hooves press
On nothing more than emptiness.
The unicorn does not exist.

    Regard the graceful, sparkling twist
    Of bone that constitutes his horn.
    It tapers to a cunning thorn.
    His eye a glowing amethyst,
    He plashes through the forest mist.

I say the unicorn, whose tail
Of tasseled fire billows, frail
As every thing that takes up space,
Does not exist, does not take place.
Even words have greater force
Than this vain, blank, unreal non-horse.
The only part of him that's true
Is that he cannot be, or do.
Lacking extension, lacking gist,
The unicorn does not exist.

    But let us speak of the unicorn:
    He wanders high grass, charmed, forlorn.
    He paws the earth, then nibbles flowers
    Between the stones of ruined towers.

And yet the unicorn is dead.
His horn has fallen from his head
And lies upon the ocean floor,
Where blind, soft sands drift, swirl, and pour.
And the ocean is no alchemist:
The unicorn does not exist.

He snorts, he paws the waves, and swims,
His horn so sharp the sunshine dims.
His great mane tangled like the foam,
He thunders free, with fierce aplomb.
Glistening, wild, he rears, then pauses —
Eyeing all the hornless clauses.

Brothers

The leaves are working the sunshine
Into innumerable presences and shadows,
And bark has overgrown the triangular blazes.
The road is many hours back.

What is this feeling hovering in the forest
I ask myself, I ask the forest,
and I ask you, for as we are here together
Perhaps we can discover it together.

Although it may be that I want to kill you,
Yes, it may be that I want to leave you here,
Dead in the forest, another Abel
As I find my way back to the city alone.

I would not murder you for any reason
Except that I do not like the way you walk
On the trail, traversing the dappled light,
Making pointless conversation in the wilderness.

And why not? I suspect that you would do the same.
I can tell by the way I catch your hungry eye
Roving across my face, or the way you become silent.
Don't pretend you haven't imagined it —

We are men and so we should acknowledge to this forest,
To the distant mountains and to the deserts beyond,
How many calm evenings are but a prelude
To defeat at the hands of shadows.

But having said that, I now know
That that is not the truth,
It is only part of the truth.
For how else could I have imagined it?

Every immeasurable passion has a past,
Like every point of the compass;
Even the trunks reaching up into the dark canopy,
Wild and silent, have names.

So Brother, walk with me: to study our own
Stubborn words, learning to sail star by star,
Choosing Gemini in every weather,
Would be a great redemption.

The Rock

Not far, but far enough away to make
The beach look like a strip of chrome,
Far enough so that the noisy break
Quiets behind its round, green back of foam,
Suspicious crabs retreat across the rock.
Some tense then hunker down in weeds to wait,
Only their stem-end eyes above the grass,
Prepared to flash their little claws at fate
If it comes clawing. Others jump. Hours pass.
The ebb tide also ebbs the world's cheap talk.

Hot, sharp, pocked granite cuts the softer foot.
Pointless, random, free, each tidal pool
Holds its small world all temporarily put,
Each creature living by its wet salt rule.
The plastic kayak bobs in the lee's shelter.
One surge-washed cleft cuts through the rock's deep center,
The long, slow work of washing winds and tides.
Blind barnacles extend their clustering welter.
A black, spiked sea anemone abides
In a fortress hollow where no tooth can enter.

Not I. I drift back gently in the sun,
First down the surging channel through the rock,
Its sloshing peace not mine, then home in one
Long swell after another, carrying talk
Back on itself. For no word is a rock.
And no one lives alone upon a rock,
Too small, too hard, too harsh and unforgiving
Even to make a bed on, let alone a living.
Ocean, paddle, wind, boat, rock – each word
Can only come to rest where songs are heard.

Would it were otherwise but it is not.
So back I go, sun dropping, as I must,
To song and all our other natural failures.

3 / The Shape of Water Most Like Love

O buono Appollo, a l'ultimo lavoro
Fammi del tuo valor sì fatto vaso,
Come dimandi a dar l'amato alloro.

O good Apollo, for this final task
Make me the vessel of your excellence,
What you, to merit your loved laurel, ask.

Paradiso 1.13-15

The Avocado

I took a run through ordered neighborhoods.
When I attained the home of my beloved,
She stood in her bright kitchen washing, cutting
Tomatoes, lettuce, peppers, mushrooms, sprouts,
And avocadoes, while sunflower seeds
And homemade mustard dressing in a bottle
Stood on the counter, ready for their work.
Playing at a drama of collapse,
I pulled my shirt and lay down on my back,
Arms spread, on the linoleum. She laughed,
She brought cool chunks of juicy avocado,
No doubt a Hass, the industry benchmark,
A breed of *Persea Americana*,
All breeds of which descend from one sweet tree
Grown in La Habra Heights, east of LA.

With a laugh, I say, she brought fresh pieces
In her small hands, cupped and dripping over,
Arranged them carefully upon my chest
Then slowly ate them, one by one. No hands.
If I had been tired I was no more.
"Don't move," she said, then leaning back looked deeply
Into my eyes and murmured…something secret.
And let me tell you, that look and those words
Have stayed, while darkness, enemy of things,
Has swallowed so much else, as it will one
Day swallow…

        …though when it does, one thing the dark
Will leave behind, indigestable
Like a diamond or a rubber boot,
For years, because I have inscribed it here,

Is how we two became so utterly
Alive via that wet, green avocado,
So alive we were almost unconscious
Of being alive, like a day itself.
For that sweet and buttery avocado
Invited fingers, kisses, more, to tangle
Like its lost roots.

                Yes, the sun gone down
Into the irrigated desert where
The avocado grew, and neighbors' lights
Now coming on, I leave you to imagine
Exactly how each laughing, fat-soaked bite
Of warm, ripe avocado goodness led us
To make love that will be well worth recalling
When all that long-gone fruit turns dust: how still
Our lips without one word are speaking great
New languages, new languages that lack
The genitive construct, in which her sweat
Was and becomes my salt and vice versa.

Admire Sandburg

Admire the wild old man, admire him, admire him,
Mocked by the priests of academies, ignored,
Muttering about steel, beauty and justice in his grave.

Admire the poor people with little shoulders
Whom he sang in his sloppy arithmetic of sympathy,
The sad, clanging, mingled, dirty mob of ordinary folks.

I say admire him, you forgetful aesthetes,
And you angry, cloistered, detached advocates of relevance,
Not for his simple chants,
Which aren't so simple, all of them, in the end,
But for the intelligence of his generosity.

He wrote to affirm, and he did it,
So difficult and admirable, out of thin air,
Singing something without which we are poor.
Admire him!

The Turn Things Take

After the boy who study's cunning makes glow
Has recognized the fact of childhood pain –
And after the sigh-kicked ale of adolescence
That loves to stand for love has ground its jaw –
After the burning pumpkin that means "burn,"
The leaping into snowy library holes,
And the overwhelming catalogue of questions –
After the need to go to the mountains forever
Has been asked again and again about its end
And never replied, and reading has revealed
Only the rhetoric of apocalypse –

That kyrie you sang so long ago
Under a dark bridge arch will also remain.
The cable-humming streets will still make sense,
Because years printed them on you, like the law
Of love that learns to take whatever turn
Things take. Stained glass bends every light to coals
Of moon, or jewel, or God and his suggestions –
And a harmony of local voices never
Was anything but love looking to bend.
There will be love, there will. The stones in a field
Themselves hear sidewalk hearts praising your lips.

Paradise Valentine

Let your eye hold my life regarding you:
I'll be the quiet fields, you be the light.
If you were someone else, I would be too.

If you became an oak, a fir, a yew,
I'd sing myself to sleep in your green height.
Let your eye hold my life regarding you.

If you became the greatest avenue,
I'd walk you back and forth from noon to night.
If you were someone else, I would be too.

I have become like truth to what is true,
Know each thing seen is only made of sight.
Let your eye hold my life regarding you.

Be language, I'll be words; be sky, I'm blue
And black and gray and red and pink and white.
If you were someone else, I would be too.

There's no relation we cannot construe –
If you became a thought I'd be its flight.
Let your eye hold my life regarding you –
If you were someone else, I would be too.

It Is Spring

"When you danced with her, you stayed danced with."
         – Fred Astaire of Cyd Charisse

It is hard to be difficult in simple spring,
When the world reknots itself, blind, daringly,
More perfect than the web bright fractals spin.
It is difficult to sit, or walk the ring
Of an eye, engaging thought as carefully
As thought demands before she lets us in

In the black-mud bud-spangled guts of spring!
Triangles lose their minds and drown in the sea,
Whose islands go wild, then wilder, with rain's romance.
Leaves finger the air. New snow dies on the wing
As rot's back breaks to set gods free
Who take the form of bodies and of plants.

Birds, beasts, and flowers open their mouths to sing.
Plural, plural, plural! chants each boundary.
Yes, many waltzes have ended, but I will dance –
For it is hard to think in simple spring.

Dandelion

At first, my love was like a single dandelion,
A lion's tooth, small sunburst in the garden,
A weed that no one ever thought to pardon.
I was the kind of man who makes hearts harden,
For I had all the manners of a dandelion.

But manners aren't the truth of love or dandelions,
Whose flowers work together, in a grand alliance,
And start to sprout up elsewhere in the lawn,
Despite whatever poison you put on.
If you could wither my love, you could handle lions.

And my true love's grown like the darling dandelion,
Worked down your field like stars strewn from the hand of Zion,
A shameless, drunk platoon of petals you can rely on
To go to seed in unrepentant bliss.
Give up! My roots exceed your artifice –
Even burnt, I'd turn sweet smoke you could stand high on.

Yes, I'm in love, and lover, it's no scandal. Spy on
My motives, go ahead and try to vandalize one –
You'll find each one as radical as a spangled ion.
Oh, let me be the one you rest your hand and eye on,
Let me sleep tangled in your arms, my manly thigh on
Your orderly borders, our love a plan to fly on.
O Lover, come lie down: I am your dandelion.

Jacob Asleep

Far from any of the many harms
That haunt the always dying world
To which he's recently been hurled,
Young Jacob snores within his father's arms.

Ignorant of almost everything,
He slowly drifts away upon
Song after song and then is gone.
What better logic could there be to sing?

Please, none of your fierce sirens and alarms –
No violated law or number,
No war ships that turn and lumber
Through dark seas, no wolves, no barren farms,

No newspapers, no rats, no sad affairs,
No failure yet at school or work,
No lonely mailman gone berserk,
No financial woes, no angry stares.

Now you must give up those cares for charms.
For the world is full of sturdy pain,
And yet there's more days must explain,
Such as a boy asleep in his father's arms.

So let spring come to country and to town.
Let his mother comb her hair.
Let him ascend from fair to fair.
Bring on the sun, let crooked dawn reach down.

In untold loneliness but warmth, with arms
That one day I hope reasoning will
Themselves more life and love fulfill,
A newborn man is sleeping in my arms.

The Child

I am a flower,
No wandering stone
On a burned-out hearth,
Or empty bone
Buried under a tower.

I am a flower,
Clutching at the up and down, comprehensible
Without one word of two-handled wit,
Blowzy with the great green jazz
Of another profit,
Stem, root, bud, pistil, stamen sensible
Within each mortal, doubling, hour.

I am a man and am an amaranth
Whose hair uncoils in victorious petals,
Who the dirt, despite exhaustion
And admonishment, will purposefully rhyme
Into a woven crown of purple buds
Punctuated by time.
Brought to the holocaust in
Ideas, or histories of precious metals,
My roots strike down again to become plant.

I am a flower,
Next to one sex the other, both
Bursting in air and advertising number,
One root and sap throwing commerce to the winds,
Rescuing tenderness and anger in a flash,
Clutching at dirt. A metaphor stuck in death's eye,
I count the openings that crash
Where dog-tired words rise and begin

To praise again the angel duration.
In the candle's work and the fluttering moth
I imagine succor.

The night, the day, and the past
Are not strong enough, and will not work
Only to break the green link between this word
And the dark sprouting of deeds.
One foot upon pavement, one in muck,
This flower riddles back the great schism
Between what is and what a flower is,
Breaks eyesight with the future's prism,
With a planting that entertains good luck,
Knows fields no matter what unleash their weeds,
That song's best overheard
Where thrushes murmur, dull toads lurk:
The full season is unencompassed.

Each one a version of the best one,
Ruling from the throne of its grass,
Which motive made the flower stand?
Which motive made death and the world
Burst with tendril, thorn, and blossom?
Discovered the engine of wild, cleft-sprung hay
As gold as sunlight, named it, and called for more?
It can only be defined as a lack.
For only no seed can come before
The first strange seed that grew a lily into day.
Only no seed could seed so far beyond its hook, awesome
In the wild garden the garden has unfurled.
In truth, the open crowd of flowers and grasses planned
Nothing, but they come, and come to pass,
Filling the hour of questions.

I am a flower.
I don't remember what I did before.
Every day I turn my face
To smile at the sun,
And when the wind blows
I wave my hands.
When the rain comes
I bow my head down,
And in the evening,
I close my petals
Around myself to sleep
Until the morning awakens me again.

The Next Poem I Will Read Is "Justified"

In general I don't like to preface readings
With explanation of any kind at all.
Poems ought to stand as they were written.
There's nothing worse than listening to some blowhard
"Explain" what you're about to hear anyhow
By talking about his or her own life,
As if anybody really cares,
Or should. Imagine Mozart doing that
While the concertmaster tunes the orchestra:
"The melody to *Eine Kleine Nachtmusik*
Came to me in a bar one soggy afternoon..."
But this next poem is an experiment,
And probably won't work, so before I read it
I'd like to say a few short words – I promise –
About the way that poetry always fails
To...articulate things in the world.

An image which has haunted me for years,
And which I've tried to write about for years,
Is what led me to the poem "Justified,"
The one I'm going to read in just a moment.
This image is one of dignity, something
You'd think could be knocked out in words
With a minimum of artifice and play.
Yet when I read the poem to myself
I can't help thinking that my lines still fail
To capture the details of what I saw —
Although that actually makes good sense to me —
There's no real reason that some thin construction
Of words and silence, or ink and empty space,
Should be able to embody life,
The actuality of our encounters,

Which are far more complex, and messier,
Than words can be and still be understood.
That's why I feel compelled to tell the story
That lurks behind this poem before I read it.

One day when I was eighteen I was waiting
In the old Greyhound terminal in Boston.
It's long gone now. This place was like a haven
For an entire generation of bums,
Old guys who looked like they had gotten lost
Sometime in the 1930s and decided
Never to come back. They'd fall asleep
Snoring on the benches, or sit there drunk,
Clutching rot-gut bottles in rumpled bags,
Indifferently pissing on themselves and begging.
You'd sometimes catch one puking in the men's room,
Drooling, one hand on a filthy sink.
As a group, they fit the part so perfectly
They looked like they'd been hired for the job.

On this day, one guy who looked really gone
Was begging by the door out to the buses.
One of the passengers, a man in a coat,
That's all I remember, without the slightest glance
Away from the door and bus that waited in the rain
To take him somewhere, quickly pressed a bill
He'd folded up into a tiny square
Into the other's palm. I couldn't figure why.
It didn't make any sense — why hide your charity?
Why pretend you didn't do what was
A manifestly generous thing to do?

As far as I know, I was the only one
Who saw this happen. Even the bum didn't know
It had occurred until he realized what
He held. By then the man was out the door.

Then something in me saw what had transpired —
The passenger had acted in this way
So one man didn't have to repay charity
With gratitude, pressed by attention's stone
To acknowledge and reiterate despair
In public. The passenger did not avoid
The ruined eyes to separate himself
From a broken man — rather he justified
His faith in the gift, and thereby magnified it,
Doing his best to respect another life,
Short circuiting all chance for thanks.
I saw he'd done his best to hide his work
From everyone, including me, who witnessed
This quiet event by chance, and memorized it
From the far side of a filthy, crowded room.
It was a graceful thing, an artifice
That showed so many other things their place.

I've tried to grasp the sense of that event
In the poem you're about to hear, but doubtless,
Because I am a poet and therefore
An exhibitionist, I'll fail to slip
It past you with the same sweet, real panache
Of that justified man in the bus station,
So you can find yourself surprised by grace,
Acknowledging your neighbors have the will
To find the way to be cunningly good.
Or do you believe you can't imagine that?

The Shape of Water Most Like Love

Rain is not the shape of water most like love,
For rain nourishes fields
Or destroys them with indifferent passion.
The sky wears rain on its sleeve.
Powerful and beautiful, but capricious,
Requiring rainbows to reassure us,
Rain is not love, only a love affair.

The ocean is not the shape of water most like love,
For it is love's destination.
Although the realm of birth, each ocean touches
Every shore and action, named or not.
A form of everything,
Yet unable to create more of itself,
The ocean is not love –
Love is but one part of its history.

Ice is not the shape of water most like love,
For ice is like what is called thinking,
A patient architecture made from what already exists.
Mostly at opposite poles, or high on rock,
Ice is not love – it broods too far away
To discover anything greater than itself.

Lakes are too inward, rivers divide.
Crystals of snow all break and decay.
Clouds and fog by definition drift.

Even at the origins, where, inhuman,
It collects as the residue of stupendous explosions,
Hurtles through emptiness in primordial comets,
Smashes into swirling tides of magma
And then later falls as first rain on mere rock,
We will not find the shape of water most like love.

What then is the shape of water most like love?
Dark hurtling molecules, interstellar balls of ice,
Clouds of steam, rain untouched by the living,
Hurricanes, unmeasured depths, and polar caps
Only churn what this collects and channels,
The drops reformed one by one, again and again,
Under irresistible darkness and force.

And you, who are mostly water,
In your unrelenting solitude coupled with movement,
Although you might do anything,
Still resemble a spring
More than you resemble a comet, or a drop of rain,
Or an ocean, or an immense distant river of ice.

What Must Be Done Again Today

It was a time of happiness. Each day
The sky would open like a great blue wing.
At night rain fell, a gentle rain. We walked,
Just to feel the water on our skin.
You could almost hear the pastures drinking.
It seemed there was a wedding every weekend,
Musicians and flirtations and delight.

It was a time of joy and olives. Old buildings
Were giving up their wasted walls for new.
Whatever we believed in we began.
Cracked plaster fell to laughter and our work.
The broken bones were slowly growing back
Together in the city's injured ankle.

It was a time of wine and song. The fact
That it was not could not destroy that fact.
For underneath a skepticism's wheel
Is the road on which it rolls. The cold cry "No!"
Is still a word, a desert still a place.
Somehow, together, we dreamed of milk
And honey, sun and working in the sun.

It was a time of happiness because
While each day seemed to be enough to fill
Itself, it also would go spilling over
Into the next, and the one before, connecting
Work to work, and word to word, and even
Hunger to its end. Like dance, each one
Became much more than a way to get somewhere.

So come, my dear dead rabbis, stand and pause.
Remember us as your beards curl in patterns
Of complex sleep on disputation's pillow.
Arise from the wreckage of the past, return.
Close your books and recognize yourselves,

Return to your senses, I conjure you, join us.
Come singing from your raptures for the dead.
Come with your questioning eyes and tapping fingers,
Your crooked fingernails and curious spirits
Which dance in circling waves of commentary.
Stand murmuring, make holy convocation,

And swear to satiate your souls with fatness.
Then let me ask you this: if not now, when?
We bow to you, our bodies bent like the bow
That fires light back from nowhere into nothing,
Because this is the time for praise, a praise
That sings beyond the genius of denials,
A praise for that which is, where we must go
If we would say even a single word.

Listen: there still is time for happiness.
Help to wipe the sorrow from our brows,
If only the better to know it for what it is.
Then lend your hands, forge keys, unlock the world,
The very world where we have made mistakes,
Where everyone has made such sad mistakes.
For who would deny that he has made mistakes?
Do not give up, let us try to understand,
To draw a map in words instead of blood.

Then, my sages, we could drink water and:
Consider here the life that makes more life.
Our hands are on those leafy branches now.
Respond to the living dust you call to praise
And inquire what must be done again today.
Let the dead instruct the living, the living the dead.
Help us to know what we already know –
That a time of happiness can come to be.

About the Author

David J. Rothman is Director of the Poetry Concentration in the MFA at Western State Colorado University, and also teaches at the University of Colorado at Boulder, Denver University, and Lighthouse Writers Workshop of Denver. He is the author of three previous volumes of poetry, *Dominion of Shadow*, *The Elephant's Chiropractor* (a Finalist for the Colorado Book Award), and *Beauty at Night*. Another volume of poems, *Part of the Darkness*, is forthcoming from Entasis and a further, Go *Big*, is forthcoming from Red Hen Press. He is the editor of *The Geography of Hope: Poets of Colorado's Western Slope*. His essays on many subjects have appeared widely. He was co-founder and the first Executive Director of the Crested Butte Music Festival, and has served as director of a number of other arts and educational organizations. He lives in Boulder, Colorado, with his wife and two sons.